Write a Captiv

Don't Bore Your History to Death – Add Context to the Story

Gary W. Clark

MW01615793

Write A Captivating Family History

Don't Bore Your History to Death – Add Context to the Story

Copyright © 2015 by Gary W. Clark

www.phototree.com

Published by PhotoTree.com

9 8 7 6 5 4 3 2 1

All rights reserved. No part of this book may be reproduced or transmitted in any form by any means, electronic, mechanical, photocopying, recording, or otherwise, without the prior written permission of the publisher, except by a reviewer who may reference short excerpts in a review. Phototree.com is a trademark of Gary W. Clark.

All images, unless otherwise noted, are the property of Gary W. Clark. For reproduction rights contact info@phototree.com

Cover photograph: Bronze statue of a boy and girl reading a book, Carnegie Library, Perry, Oklahoma. Titled "A Great Story . . . Then and Now". Sculpture by Jim Franklin. Photo by Gary Clark.

ISBN: 978-0-9907615-4-9

Cover and interior design by Gary W. Clark

Edited by Gena Philibert-Ortega

Dedication

This book is dedicated to everyone that takes the first step, no matter how intimidating, to writing his or her family history. Preserving family stories, tales, and recording our ancestors' way of life for future generations is a noble effort.

Gary W. Clark

Contents

Introduction

A new and admirable movement in genealogy and family history circles is to write one's family story; not just record the names, dates, and places of ancestors and events.

We diligently look for, find, and record our ancestor's birth dates, spouse and offspring information, and relationships with others. Yet so often, stories of their dreams, struggles, accomplishments, failures, happiness, and sadness are overlooked. Many of these are found in family stories, but usually only in verbal tales shared with a small number of people. Do not let these stories die from neglect.

Start now. Write down the family tales. Discuss your ancestor's personalities and actions with those who remember them. Then, when you are ready, compile the stories into a book.

Your actions and revelations may inspire others in your family to take an interest in the past. An exciting story may attract the interest of younger family members also; trust me, there is nothing more boring to a teenager than a *Family Group Sheet.*

However, if you told that same youngster their great-great-grandfather went west in a covered wagon across barren prairies, fearing for their lives from drought, blizzards, raids, or any number of challenges; they may look up with bright eyes. Whether working in steel mills at the turn of century, farming behind a team of horses, coming into Ellis Island, living during two world wars, and witnessing countless life-changing inventions – our ancestors were very interesting people; each with unique experiences and stories.

I will offer many tips, tricks, ideas, and suggestions to help you draw out narratives surrounding your ancestors' lives.

When to Start Writing Your Book

Writing is not dependent on you completing a genealogical record. I have a great-great-grandfather that was a very interesting person, starting with his name; Orange Clark. He was a pioneer into the Midwest, traveled to California for the gold rush, homesteaded throughout Kansas and Oklahoma; yet we still do not know of his last few years, where he died, and where he is buried. However, his story is written up to the time we know. It just ends in a mystery.

Write what you do know. You may find that exercise will help you look elsewhere and find more information. I am not promoting a popular online genealogy company, though they do have a nice catch phrase: "You don't have to know what you are looking for, just start looking." Same with writing your stories; you may not know the ending, but just start writing what you know.

What Is This Book About?

I hope to help you write an interesting story. A story that will give the reader an indepth sense of the person in your history. I will give you some ideas, tips, and tricks to make your writing a compelling read. The greatest compliment I received from my most recent book, *Cruel Irony*, was how I told my ancestor's stories in context with the world and time around them.

Gary W. Clark
PhotoTree.com

Chapter 1

But I ~~Can't~~ Cannot Write ~~Good~~ Well

Medieval Writing Desk (Wikimedia Commons)[1]

Do not worry about it, for now. It is most important to record events, stories, and family lore before they are lost. In addition, the act of writing the stories may trigger more stories or cause you to seek clarification from others. You will find the act of writing may lead you to a cascading series of stories you had not thought of. Individual stories, when knitted together will make for great reading.

This Book is NOT About Grammar

Nor is it about spelling, or sentence structure, or past participle conjunctive verbs. Ok, that last phrase is nonsense. You will need a different book on those topics. However, do not let the challenges of writing fundamentals stop you. After you have written a piece the best you can, enlist some editing assistance from relatives or friends. Or, one inexpensive source for editing assistance is your local college; many advanced English majors and graduate students take on editing work to make a little money. Check with the English department or school newspaper.

Also, there is a website named fiverr.com that connects everyday people who need a creative service with specialists in that field for a very reasonable price. As of this writing, numerous ads were posted for editing stories of 2,500 to 5,000 words, for only $5.00. (For reference, this book is about 7,500 words.) Also, editors in your area probably can be found with a Google search; use the search term copy editor [your city].

If you are a member of a local genealogical or historical society, ask if any members perform such services.

This Book is NOT About Genealogy Research

Whether you have invested years in research and collection of family history, or only have stories passed down through generations, start writing now. Research is never done, so do not wait until you think it is to start putting your history into story form.

This book is not intended to help or guide you through research. There are plenty of books, classes, and conferences about finding ancestors and breaking through brick walls.

It is About Making Your Story Interesting

This book will help you weave an interesting story. You would be surprised how knowing the weather, economic and political climate, occupational experiences, living conditions, society pressures, and other forces can help expand the story of your grandparent's lives in 1927. Today, all that information is easily obtained.

Don't Be Afraid to Rewrite Your Words

You may want or need to rewrite your words many times. Actually, one of my favorite books over the years has been *Getting The Words Right, How to Rewrite, Edit, and Revise,* by Theodore A. Rees Cheney. I bought it over 20 years ago and still refer to it occasionally.

You Too Can Be a Hemingway

Ernest Hemingway rewrote the ending to his classic book "Farwell to Arms" 47 times. When he was asked by George Plimpton of the Paris Review what had been the reason for so many endings, Hemingway replied: *"Getting the words right."*

My guess is that Mr. Cheney borrowed Hemingway's words for his book title. At the very least, it is an interesting coincidence.

Links

1   https://commons.wikimedia.org/wiki/File:Medieval_writing_desk.jpg

Chapter 2

Set the Stage for Your Story

You have the power to direct the story; telling it in a captivating manner while keeping true to the facts. Make use of everything available to you.

Details, commentary, and life conditions that surrounded your family history are found everywhere. When writing stories, we tend to rely strictly on a living ancestor's memory, written documents such as letters and diaries, and maybe tales told around the dinner table or at family reunions.

Yet, these sources usually only focus on the most prominent portion of a story, and reveal little of the setting or independent events that may have influenced the main story.

First, Craft the Story

You have some raw information, now is the time to make it a good read. I will show you how to strengthen, add context, and make your story fun to read by incorporating information about:

- » Historical weather
- » Political and social climate
- » Economics and standard of living
- » Historic advertisements
- » Workplaces
- » Friends, co-workers, distant relatives
- » Life on the farm or in the city
- » Schools and education
- » Movie and book influence
- » Politics, elections, wars
- » Contemporary celebrities
- » Company employment
- » Unions and fraternal organizations
- » Local history and events

In my most recent book, *Cruel Irony*, I included the above subjects as they pertained to my story, to create an engaging family history that chronicled the life of one person among my ancestors. It became a story of more than just where the main character went, what she did, where she worked, when she died. Writing about simple facts would have made for a boring read.

By intertwining her actions with the surrounding world at the time made for an interesting setting, and possibly explained some of the values she possessed and actions she took.

Missing Pieces

Frequently, pertinent events, people's actions, or motivations are missing from a family story. Sometimes unsubstantiated family lore has spawned a mystery. If rumors, tales, and whispered secrets were a part of explaining events, then these were actually part of the family history. Do not ignore them, yet portray them honestly by not claiming absolute fact. Consideration should be given to cause no harm to the living.

This can be a tricky area in writing family history, and experts disagree about writing such information. However, by preserving speculations or third-hand stories, these words may help solve questions much later as new evidence turn up, or other pieces of the puzzle fall into place. Be sure to label what is conjecture and speculation, attributing as much fact or circumstantial evidence to it as possible.

Show and Tell

In this book, I use real, specific examples from a family story to illustrate suggestions or tips.

I recently published *Cruel Irony – Triumphs and Tragedies of a Modern Woman*. The book weaves the history of early Kansas pioneers and their tales of hardship and tragedy, with the life of a pivotal person in the family. The blended story offer solutions to many previously unanswered family questions. Additionally, it tells a compelling story in context to the era.

Cruel Irony

Tragedies and Triumphs of a Modern Woman.

Available from Amazon.com

Sources of Rich Information

First-hand information adds a personal touch to any story, and may reveal tales that rival any gripping fictional story.

Family Memories

Sometimes the most detailed and fascinating information is at hand, yet we overlook it; our living family. Reach out to grandparents, aunts, uncles, distant cousins, and even neighbors of your ancestors for stories and tales that will never be found in your favorite online database.

From experience, I know that it will be fruitless to ask them general questions about the past, something like tell me what it was like to grow up on a farm. Or how bad was the Depression? Their mind will not know where to start, and hence nothing specific will come out.

Ask questions like; *how did you get to school? How often could you take a bath? Where did your father work during the depression? What did you do for entertainment? Did you have a garden?*

Jokingly, I recently told my Aunt Margaret, one of the key characters in *Cruel Irony,* that she frustrated me so much because I could not just ask her everything she knew and have it pour out. However, every time I visited her she told me new and surprising stories not divulged before. To help prime the memory pump, before I saw her I would think of topics or specific questions to ask. Then by memory association, a fresh stream of stories usually bubbled to the surface when we talked.

Public Data

Sources in family research can also yield a larger picture about a specific topic you explored.

For example, you have found your ancestor's Civil War, World War I, World War II, or even Vietnam draft record, but what was the national and local attitude towards the draft and the conflict driving conscription? How did that draft come into being? How many men were drafted? What were the criteria?

This type of information is available from any number of newspaper stories and even books written on the topic. Your ancestors were emotionally invested in these events; set the stage so your reader can understand the sentiments of the time.

Let the Writing Fun Begin

The following chapters will show how and why to include the bigger picture into your story, making it a compelling read for your family and possibly the general public.

Chapter 3

Local Conditions: Sunny with Rain

Wichita Eagle, Nov. 30, 1907 (Newspapers.com)

It was a dark and stormy night! No, do not use this, even though the Peanuts cartoon character Snoopy opened each of his novels with the time worn cliché.

However, do talk about weather conditions that occurred during your story. Of course, use this trick sparingly, not with every event lest your readers think you have a Weather Channel fetish. This works well when the weather is especially important to the occasion. It helps the reader envision the scene and appreciate the character's situation and maybe their state of mind.

If you are describing a particular event:

- » What is the current season?
- » Are they likelybundled up or wearing light clothing?
- » What was the temperature that day or week?
- » Did that impact the activity?
- » Are they recovering from a bad winter or scorching summer?
- » How was their horse and buggy, car, house or workplace able to cope with the weather?
- » Did the event involve travel?

» Were the roads impassable due to weather?
» Did the weather result in illness or death?

Weather dictated our ancestor's actions much more that it does today. In sub-freezing weather, you were less likely to frequent distant places, even a general store, in a drafty Model T or open carriage than if it was a nice warm day. Today, we just turn on the car's seat warmer and away we go.

Example of Including Weather

This passage from *Cruel Irony* describes an ancestor's trip from their farm into town – in November.

Saturday, November 30, 1907 would be a great day to ride into Winfield, just four miles away. The prior day's temperature reached the lower 50s, this day was to be even warmer. This mild weather was a bit unusual for late November; it might be the last warm day of the year for an enjoyable trip to the big town. The whole family would take advantage of the trip, including mother Marian, Esther and two of her sisters Inez and Mina, brother Willie, and father William.

In this case, the weather may have allowed the trip to happen, or even encouraged it. It was November in Kansas; the day should have been quite brisk, if not cold. So why did this trip even matter? The father would die of a heart attack in the town's barber shop that day.

Finding the Weather

Discovering weather reports is usually easy and can be found from a number of places, including weather history websites, online digitized historical newspapers, and microfilmed newspaper copies in your local library.

Google

A typical Google (or your favorite search engine) search for past weather might be formatted like this:

Winfield, KS weather November 9, 1907

Of course, substitute your city and desired date. Some local resources may give detailed data. This may not always give you ideal results, but it is worth a try; also try other variations of search terms.

Weather Underground

This website lets you check the weather back to 1945 by city and state or zip code. It gives the basic data but no descriptive information like "worst snow storm in ten years."

http://www.wunderground.com/history/

Newspapers.com

This is a great place to find complete newspapers from across the country. Look for articles about the weather conditions during your story timeframe. Access to past newspapers is by a reasonable subscription fee; if you have a short-term project, an economical monthly rate is available.

www.Newspapers.com

Chapter 4

Political and Social Climate

Theodore Roosevelt salutes crowd (Library of Congress)

Did issues in political and social arenas affect the lives of your ancestors?

Why include this type of discussion? Well, your reader may relate to your ancestor's story by associating it with a timeframe they are familiar with or remember. It is possible, that historical events influenced your ancestor's life.

Does your story take place in any of these eras?

- » 1860s Civil War and Reconstruction
- » 1870s Long Depression, droughts & grasshoppers
- » 1880s Little Ice Age
- » 1890s Industrial Revolution

- » 1900s   Spanish American War
- » 1910s   World War I, draft
- » 1920s   Prohibition, Roaring Twenties
- » 1930s   Great Depression, Nazi rise in Europe
- » 1940s   World War II, rationing, and post boom
- » 1950s   Baby boom and prosperity, Red Scare
- » 1960s   Space race, Vietnam, and race riots
- » 1970s   Peace movements, Disco

Many of the above topics had profound impact on our ancestors and their stories. How they coped with some of these events, and many others, gives insight into their character, priorities, motives, and actions.

The following provides insight into the father of *Cruel Irony's* main character, by putting the era into perspective.

Bill scratched out a meager living with odd jobs until he swallowed his pride and took a WPA job in 1939, building bridges in the area.

The Work Projects Administration was an enormous government program that provided millions of workers with income during the depression. Conservative stalwarts like Bill were opposed to many government programs, and he was noticeably critical of the new Social Security program in an interview by the Wichita Eagle newspaper in December 1936. Still, he was responsible for feeding fourteen mouths and more would arrive on schedule. The older kids in the family pitched in financial support also; Bill's oldest daughter Mina worked at the local telephone exchange, and his teenage son Marvin actually made more than Bill in 1939, a whopping $700 as a gro-

> *cery store clerk. Bill only made $360 for 32 weeks work with the WPA.*

Details of Bill's work were not part of any family stories passed down after his death; it was simply known he worked for the Works Progress Administration (WPA). Well, that would have taken one sentence to convey and would not provide much context. With a little research, interesting details emerged.

The 1940 U.S. census revealed he worked for the WPA and even how much he made in 1939. Family heirlooms included a newspaper article from 1936 where his opinion of the new Social Security program was less than favorable.

With this additional information, we see that his family responsibilities came first. This gives a glimpse of his character to those who never knew him; this is now a part of his personal story.

This is just one example, at one point in time. The inclusion and impact of current events throughout a family history will help give your writing and your family history some depth.

Wartime Events

Wartime affects not only soldiers and sailors, but also the people at home. During World War I, there was a major push for people to join the Red Cross. Were your ancestors members?

World War II stories of the home folk include the use of ration books and coupons for critical foods and goods; many books and coupons still exist in family collections. Research how rationing affected their daily lives. Did they grow 'victory' gardens?

Kids would scour the neighborhood for cans and other re-cyclables and turn them in for war materials. Even disposable cooking oil or grease was collected for use in manufacturing explosives.

A frequently heard phrase was *Bacon to Bullets.* The government produced one poster that included an image of a large canon with the headline reading: **For Gunpowder - SAVE WASTE FATS - Rush Them to Your Meat Dealer**.

Are any related stories in your family history?

Chapter 5

Economics and Standard of Living

1920s children on a Reno County, Kansas farm. (Gary Clark collection)

We've all heard from members of older generations that back in my day a loaf of bread was only a nickel! Or, a gallon of gas was 25¢. Or, I worked for $1.15 a day.

Well, all that was true. However, what did it mean in context? The dollar certainly went further in days past. Without a time machine, it seems impossible to understand the value of money and goods compared to today.

However, there is an app for that. There are numerous currency value websites that can give you a sense of the value of a monetary amount in the past.

Futureboy Currency Calculator

Futureboy.us is the simplest calculator, and arrives at a similar value as many more complicated websites. You simply enter a dollar amount (or choose a number of currencies), from a past year, and it will calculate today's value

http://futureboy.us/fsp/dollar.fsp

Measuringworth.com

This calculator offers a number of different results that reflect purchasing power, consumer price index, standard of living, and economic status. Again, you enter an original year and amount, but then you can enter a year to compare it to, not just today's value. This is an entertaining exercise.

http://www.measuringworth.com/uscompare/

Using Converted Currency

How could this be useful in your family history writings you ask? Good question. Some interesting comparisons to past values can help understand your ancestor's way of life. Use this to see today's value of:

>> Property and inheritance from wills and probate records.
>> Value of land transactions from county records.
>> Military pension amounts.
>> Wages listed in census, and other records.
>> Any money values you find in family documents.

I was able to find annual reports from the Upper Canada Bible

Society from the 1860s that detailed the salary of the main character's grandfather in *Cruel Irony*.

I converted Canadian pounds at the time to dollars, and them calculated a present value. All this returned some interesting results.

To be clear, his position with the Bible Society paid him very well. The Society's annual reports detailed the year's accounting, not just for small expenses, but agent salaries as well. Stephen Johnson was frequently the highest paid person on the Upper Canada Bible Society staff. Some years he was paid over 1,200 Canadian pounds, which translated to U.S. dollars, then converted to present-day wealth, his annual salary would be approximately $90,000.

This was quite a surprise to the current family. Most accounts of the family going back several hundred years was that our ancestors were usually poor. However, during this time they were able to move to the United States and acquire farm property and equipment quite easily. It was always a mystery, until his income and value of it was revealed. This certainly made the story more interesting and enlightening.

Chapter 6

Advertisements, Celebrities, and Authors

Amelia Earhart (Stanford School of Medicine)[1]

Newspapers are one of the greatest sources from which you can harvest fantastic content. Stories written during an era you are describing can add so much perspective to your own words. You can use national or local publications, from any number of sources.

In addition to commentary, magazines can contribute topical artwork or photographs to your story. You must take into account copyrighted material, but there are many copyright-free sources. (Appendix B lists some helpful information on copyright concerns.)

In *Cruel Irony,* I was trying to express how the pressures of 1920s society influenced the main character's actions and habits. As a young college girl at the time, she was definitely susceptible to slick advertising; as in the example above, Amelia Earhart advertising Lucky Strike cigarettes. I searched the internet for cigarette advertisements and found a variety of ads featuring Hollywood stars, Miss America, and of course Amelia Earhart.

Men had smoked for more than a couple of centuries, but society frowned upon the sight of women puffing on a cigarette. The act needed to be elegant. Glamorous celebrities added grace to the habit with long stylish cigarette holders that doubled as fashion accessories. The cigarette industry stepped up its advertising in the 1920s with ads targeting women; using celebrities such as Jean Harlow, Miss America, and even Amelia Earhart. After Miss Earhart's participation in the high-publicized 1928 Atlantic Ocean crossing, cigarette maker Lucky Strike created a daring advertisement illustrated with a large photo of Miss Earhart wearing flight gear and the quote:

"Lucky Strikes were the cigarettes carried on the 'Friendship' when she crossed the Atlantic."

It was prominently signed: "*Amelia M. Earhart, First woman to fly the Atlantic by aeroplane.*"

This was important to the story, as her brother banished her from the family because her unlady-like habits, including smoking, were a bad influence on his kids.

References do not have to be controversial; they could show the price of a newly purchased car or tractor.

Celebrity Influence

People of all eras were influenced by celebrities. Before the talkies, it was primarily authors that affected thought, though stage stars were also followed and adored. However, motion pictures gave celebrity worship a major boost of popularity. Handsome men and elegant women from early films influenced social values, style, and habits. Who did your ancestor's idolize?

Uncle Marvin and his Clark Cable pose. (Gary Clark collection.)

One of my uncles was a dead ringer for Clark Gable in the early 1940s. As a dashing WWII fighter pilot he sported a thin mustache and slicked hair exactly like Gable, drove a classy or sporty car, and always posed in dramatic fashion. I cannot believe it was pure coincidence.

This is the type of observation worthy of inclusion in the family history book.

In *Cruel Irony*, the heroine Esther was greatly influenced by the Roaring Twenties. She was a fan of current movie stars and starlets; naming her cat after a silent film leading man. Many of her photographs give glimpses of her taking on the persona of a dramatic scene she probably admired.

Esther, from *Cruel Irony,* in a dramatic pose. (Gary Clark collection)

Esther could mimic much of the era's drama in personal photographs, delivering a theatrical pose worthy of any movie scene.

Style and fashion became more practical, yet delivered an unmistakable and unique flair to the 1920s. Bobbed hair, straight-line dress cuts, and hats that would be considered unfeminine just ten years earlier, defined the flapper look. Esther pulled off these looks with ease; her slim frame accentuated the current designs.

Our ancestors did not have to follow the movies; styles were admired and copied from magazines and catalogs. The *Gibson Girl* look, created by renowned illustrator Charles Dana Gibson in the late 1890s, influenced women's styles for nearly two decades.

One of my favorite sources for styles is old mail order catalogs. I frequently refer to a 1896 *Sears, Roebuck* mail order catalog to find items available in the era and their prices.

Links

1   http://171.67.24.121/tobacco_web/images/tobacco_ads/targeting_women/mass_marketing_begins/large/mass_marketing_9.jpg

Chapter 7

Impact of Historical Changes

Two modes of transportation in 1916. (Gary Clark collection)

No matter how far into the past we look, our ancestors saw many dramatic changes that we take for granted. Imagine the conversations that occurred around the kitchen table, in churches, or on the streets about:

- » Introduction of the steam engine.
- » The War Between the States.
- » March of the iron horse towards the west.
- » Free land through homesteading.
- » Introduction of the automobile.
- » Introduction of electricity and telephones.
- » Indoor water and bathrooms.
- » Jet airliners.
- » Post WWII appliances and boom.

In your writing, discuss some of the dramatic changes that may have altered your ancestor's lives. For example, conduct local research as to when public electricity became available. Ask older relatives questions of what they remember about specific lifestyle changes.

Several years ago at a family reunion, I asked a couple aunts, born in the 1930s, how often and how they took baths when they were young kids. My mother grew up in a very small town, part of a poor household, with many siblings; fourteen to be exact. The family did not have an indoor bathroom until the 1950s. The aunts were not embarrassed, even a bit proud of their hardships, and told me frankly the schedule was once a week, in a galvanized tub with hot water from the stove. Oh, several small kids were in the tub at one time! All of this goes in the family history book.

Do not be bashful asking questions; tactful, but not bashful. You may hear stories of heated bricks taken to bed in the winter to keep their feet warm, and stuffing rags around the windows and doors during dust storms to keep the blowing dirt out.

In *Cruel Irony,* I discussed a family trip from the farm into town in 1907. The family, including my grandfather who was fourteen at the time, did not have a car; there were only about 100 registered in the largest nearby city. While researching the book I found a list of registered automobiles in a 1907 city directory. Little pieces of information like this can add meaningful tidbits to your story.

The younger kids in the family would probably have been excited about going to the big town of Winfield, Kansas with more than 5,000 residents.

Winfield was approaching 6,000 inhabitants and bustled with a vibrant downtown and variety of stores and business. Electric lines were strung throughout town and mule drawn trolleys provided public transportation around the sprawling town. Maybe Esther and Willie could even get a glimpse of an automobile, still a rarity in small towns; the big city of Wichita, forty miles north, had only 106 registered cars

---

While children were probably thrilled at the sight of powered automobiles, even the adults had to sense that a dramatic change was approaching.

Look for historical and interesting changes in a number of places.

» Local newspaper archives can reveal specific stories of your ancestors' surroundings. Even distant, large city newspapers can still give you a picture of where the country was heading at the time.

» Many cities, large or small, have been fortunate to be the subject of detailed histories written about them. Seek out these books; they help with your story.

» Arcadia Publishing (www.arcadiapublishing.com) has built a successful business by publishing histories of even the smallest towns and areas within larger cities. They enlist local historians to write the book, and publish interesting, professional works. See if your area is in their online catalog.

Chapter 8

Rural and Farm Lives

Family with horse drawn wagon in 1920s Kansas. (Gary Clark collection)

According to a 2000 U.S. Department of Agriculture (USDA) report, in 1900, 41% of the workforce was employed in agriculture. 1930 saw this number drop to 21.5%; 1945, 16%; 1970, 4 percent, and by the year 2000 only 1% of the U.S. population worked in agriculture.

Obviously, the further back in time we look, more of the population worked on farms or in related occupations.

» In conjunction with population censuses, the U.S. produced Non-Population Schedules for agriculture, industry, and manufacturing. These schedules recorded livestock counts and produce amounts, along with acreage and other data. Those censuses produced from 1850 to 1880 can be found on databases such as Ancestry.com[1]. Complete agriculture census information is available from the U.S. Census Bureau[2].

33

» Some states conducted an agricultural census, which recorded the number of acres of specific crops, animal head counts, and other data on each farm. Some of these censuses even listed the number of dogs on the farm. These were usually conducted in the middle of the decade (e.g. 1885); see if your state used these.

If this data is available, discuss how your ancestors were able to maintain such a farm with the known family size. Farm children typically were responsible for completing a number of chores in the morning before they left for school.

» Old plat maps can help you pinpoint a farm. Part of your rural family's story could include how far they lived from town. Here is a little tip you may not have known.

As the pioneers moved west, and the agricultural states were surveyed, most counties were designed with a county seat in the middle of the county. The size of the county was dictated by the requirement that a farmer could ride his horse, or drive a wagon or buggy to the county seat and back home in one day.

The further a farm was to the county seat or a substantial town, the more isolated the families must have felt. Trips to town would have been looked forward to with great anticipation, especially by youngsters.

Rural areas saw the modern conveniences of electricity and telephone connections arrive later than their city counterparts. Try to find out via area history and newspaper reports when your rural ancestors enjoyed the services we take for granted.

Ancestor's probate records, including wills and sales of property can give a glimpse into their farming capability and assets.

If sale documents are available, use the currency value calculators mentioned earlier to get feeling for their financial situation.

Links

1 http://search.ancestry.com/search/db.aspx?dbid=1276

2 https://www.census.gov/history/www/programs/agriculture/census_of_agriculture.html

Chapter 9

Schools and Colleges

1920s rural school bus near Burrton, Kansas. (Gary Clark collection.)

I had to walk six miles to school, uphill both ways. Ok, this is a bit of a stretch, but common or similar claims have been made by our ancestors. My father actually did ride his pony to the one-room country school in Sumner County, Kansas, one with a quaint name: *Bloody Run School.*

Just as the workplace had a big impact on adults, school had a big impact on children, even beyond the book-learning part. Find out how far their school was from home; it was common for children to walk quite far. How much of a struggle would it have been getting to school in inclement weather?

The 1920s rural school bus was unusual for the time. The photo above, printed from some recently discovered negatives belonging to a great-aunt, was probably taken around Burrton, Kansas, a small town of about 650 people.

> » If the school is rural, check plat maps for markers showing school locations.
> » If the school is in the city, check old city maps if the school is not still standing.

Yearbooks, usually from high schools, are great sources of information. Some city libraries will have copies, and there are even websites that have cataloged them. You might even see if the one you are looking for is available on eBay.

Chapter 10

Church and Religious Affiliation

Strong City, KS church built in 1880. (Gary Clark collection.)

Many of our ancestors arrived in the United States as part of a group of people who immigrated together. These included whole or nearly whole congregations that ventured to the new world. Alternatively, a large number of people in an area may have left their homeland at the same time, driven by famine, political upheaval, or promises of a better life. From the 1860s to the end of the century, railroad agents traveled through Europe soliciting immigrants with promises of free land via homesteading, and freedoms from religious or political persecution.

This resulted in whole communities comprised mostly of similar people with a common religion. Many church records represent the migration of these people and wonderful stories.

Do not ignore these resources as they may hold the answers to many questions.

Well after immigration, these church records can help establish or verify where people were at a point in time, when they were born, married, baptized, and died. Combine these facts with their religious activities such as choir participation, charity work, and other involvement and your ancestor's story takes on additional and important depth.

In *Cruel Irony*, a long-told, but unconfirmed story was finally proven as fact with assistance from a local church who searched through dusty, fragile 1940s ledgers for a baptism record.

For many years, Johnson family stories included the notion that Esther converted to Catholicism. However, family members with firsthand knowledge had long-since passed away and seemingly no physical evidence remained, that would confirm or deny the story. A conversion would have been an important step in Esther's life; maybe it would enrich her peace of mind. So, a search for her conversion records was launched with the goal of finding the truth and understanding this portion of her life.

It was apparent that the St. Joseph Catholic Church in Wichita was the most likely place she would have joined the Roman Catholic faith. Its proximity to Esther's home and work places, the timing in her life, and her association with Catholic colleagues all guided the research to this church as a possibility. Family stories led her family to believe she may have joined her new faith as early as the 1920s, at the latest sometime in the 1930s.

This portion of *Cruel Irony* contributed many pages of interesting sleuthing, and finally established the facts and circumstances surrounding a previously unfounded story.

Researching church records can be daunting; the vast majority of records from small congregations are not available in digitized, online sources. However, do not be shy about visiting churches you think may harbor records of your ancestors. With kind words and clear but simple explanation of your goals, you may find church personnel very willing to help you with your research.

Numerous genealogy websites provide suggestions, guidance, and links to detailed sources. Check out these sources for information about church records research:

>> Cyndi's List – Religion and Churches[1]
>> RootsWeb's Guide to Tracing Family Trees[2]
>> Genealogy.com – Locating Church Records[3]

There are many relevant websites for church record research; Cyndi's List has a very comprehensive directory.

Links

1 http://www.cyndislist.com/religion
2 http://rwguide.rootsweb.ancestry.com/lesson17.htm
3 http://www.genealogy.com/articles/research/5_grnwd.html

Chapter 11

Occupations and Workplaces

We Can Do It by J. Howard Miller (Wikipedia)

Much can be gleaned from an ancestor's workplace or skill they possessed.

If your ancestor worked in the city, research their place of employment or occupation. If they worked for a large company, local newspapers probably published stories about the business. General economic stories can shed light on the conditions at the time also. Union activities were usually well covered by the press; was your ancestor in a union? Did your ancestors work during World War II in military-related industries?

Newspaper want ads can be a great source of information; salaries and requirements may be listed. This type of information can give your ancestor's work history some detail and insight. In addition, their occupation likely dictated their standard of living, where they lived, and their mode of transportation; all interesting topics in a family history.

Research the following subjects to help build a story around your ancestor:

- » Occupation or skill.
- » Places of employment.
- » Wages of typical work in their field.
- » Training for the job.
- » Union involvement.
- » Retirement benefits if any.
- » Distance from home.
- » Hours typically worked.
- » Working conditions.
- » Multiple jobs to support family.

A person's work usually occupied the largest portion of their day; it shaped them and their family. Do not ignore this crucial part of their lives when writing a family history narrative.

Chapter 12

Civic and Fraternal Organizations

GAR and Women's Relief Corp emblems. (Gary Clark collection)

Throughout the 19th and early 20th century, a larger share of people were involved with fraternal organizations than today. These groups were a major part of social life, performed community services, and some supported local business and trade.

Some organizations had separate men and women's groups, each supporting the other, but also having their own specific interests.

If you have evidence or family stories about your ancestor's involvement, search available internet, library, and archival records for those organizations and activities. Many times, rosters and membership lists are available. Be sure to keep any membership cards your ancestors had as they can give clues as to affiliation, dates, and places. Search local newspapers for benefits and other activities the organizations conducted. Here are some of the more common organizations to consider.

» Grand Army of the Republic (GAR) records
» Women's Relief Corp (WRC), a GAR auxiliary
» Freemasonry (Masons, Masonic)
» Order of Eastern Star, Freemason auxiliary
» International Organization of Odd Fellows (IOOF)
» Rebekah Lodge, IOOF women's auxiliary
» Modern Woodmen of America
» Veterans of Foreign Wars (VFW)
» American Legion
» Knights of Columbus
» Order of Elks
» Fraternal Order of Eagles

One of my favorites from the 1907 Wichita, Kansas City Directory is the *Anti-Horse Thief Association No. 402.* Most city directory entries also list organization officer's names.

Appendix A

Sources

These are some of the best sources of information that can help you construct a bigger story around your family history. These are sources which I found the most relevant and easy to use.

My Favorites

» Newspapers.com – Online access to old newspapers throughout the U.S. (greatest selection) and the world. This is my go-to source for a look at both local and national history. Ancestry.com – This is an amazing collection of records from census; marriage, birth, and death records; immigration; military, and too many categories to list.

» The city public library for local newspaper microfilm. While not as convenient as an online resource, you may find past stories here that are not available online.

» State and Local Historical Societies -These may have local newspapers (digital, microfilm, actual) that provide historical context.

» Library of Congress (LOC) – While this is an enormous repository of information, learn how to navigate it and you may find fantastic images, reports, stories, and data to help your story.

» Google – Try searching for specific information relative to your story. Use a year designation in the search (e.g. 1920, 1920s). Your favorite search engine, such as Bing.com, works well also.

» Wikipedia – Though this is not focused on specific news of a certain day or timeframe (except for big events), you should look here for places and events.

Additional Resources

» FamilySearch.com – This is a free website of genealogy research material from the Church of Jesus Christ of Latter-day Saints (Mormons).

» Fold3.com – A subsidiary of Ancestry.com, this website is focused on military records.

» MyHeritage.com – Another source of genealogy records with exceptional strength in the U.K. and Europe.

» GenealogyBank – An online resource for U.S. newspaper.

» Wikepedia Commons – Largely copyright-free images useful for illustrating your writings.

Appendix B

Copyright Tips

The internet has thrown much confusion into the understanding of copyright laws. I do not present the definitive answer to your copyright questions here, but do offer some sources to consult.

Since many of the tips offered in the book deal with information gleaned from newspapers, magazines, websites, libraries, and other sources, the law may apply differently to not only each category, but each source, and sometimes to each document.

Copyright Resources

> » The U.S. Copyright Office has produced an excellent guide (PDF) on Copyright Basics.[1] I highly recommend you read this document; it will answer many of your copyright questions
> » U.S. Copyright Office page, FAQ[2]
> » The Library of Congress has a comprehensive page on copyright information, mainly as it applies to their website[3]

Note: All images in this book are the property of and copyrighted by Gary W. Clark, except where specifically labeled. All my owned pictures are either ancestors or photographs taken by ancestors. Yes, I am very lucky to have such a collection.

Links

1   http://www.copyright.gov/circs/circ01.pdf

2   http://www.copyright.gov/help/faq/

3   http://www.loc.gov/rr/print/195_copr.html

Books by Gary Clark

Photography

Photo Restoration
A Step-by-Step Guide for Repairing Photographs with Photoshop Elements.

19th Century Card Photos
A Step-by-Step Guide to Identifying and Dating Cartes de Visite and Cabinet Cards.

Cased Images and Tintypes
A Guide to Identifying and Dating Daguerreotypes, Ambrotypes, and Tintypes.

Real Photo Postcards
A Guide to Identifying and Dating Real Photo Postcards of the 20th Century.

Archive Photography
How to photograph oversize photos, curled documents, and heirloom treasures.

Gravestone Photography and Documentation
Document ancestor graves with photographs and location data.

Slides and Negatives
Digitize and Protect Your Vintage Film.

Historical

Fubar 2.0
A Soldier's Insight into Military Chaos

Cruel Irony
Triumphs and Tragedies of a Modern Woman

All books available from Amazon.com

Author Biography

I am a professional photographer, graphic designer, and genealogist who has merged those pursuits and now share the knowledge, techniques, and skills I have learned with others.

My *KwikGuide* series of books help genealogists, family historians, and photograph collectors understand their photographs by determining when the photos were made and by which technique. In addition, a photo restoration book guides the readers through digital repairs of damaged photographs.

The *Home Archivist* series of books help you capture and document historical information from cemeteries, old photos and negatives, historical documents, and heirloom items.

2015 saw the introduction of a new book: *Cruel Irony: Triumphs and Tragedies of a Modern Woman*. A true story of woman born on the prairies of Kansas in 1896 who saw many changes in the world and herself, it brings the era's history to a real person. *Cruel Irony* also suggests a captivating way to tell a family history story.

My Amazon author page tells of current interests and new books: **www.amazon.com/author/gary-clark.**

In addition, my website www.PhotoTree.com provides a wealth of free information about vintage photographs. For nearly twenty years, this site has been a great source of photograph information for genealogists and family historians

Gary W. Clark
gary@phototree.com

Made in the USA
Las Vegas, NV
13 November 2022

59338960R00030